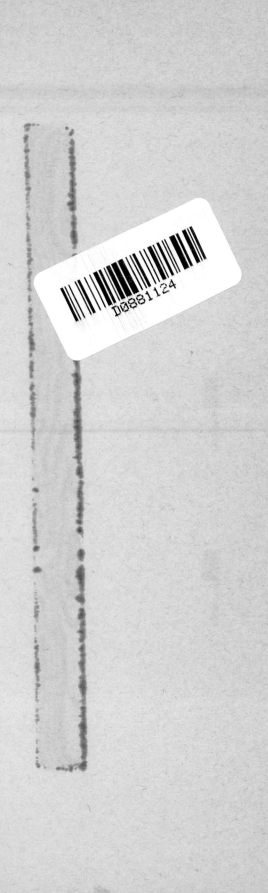

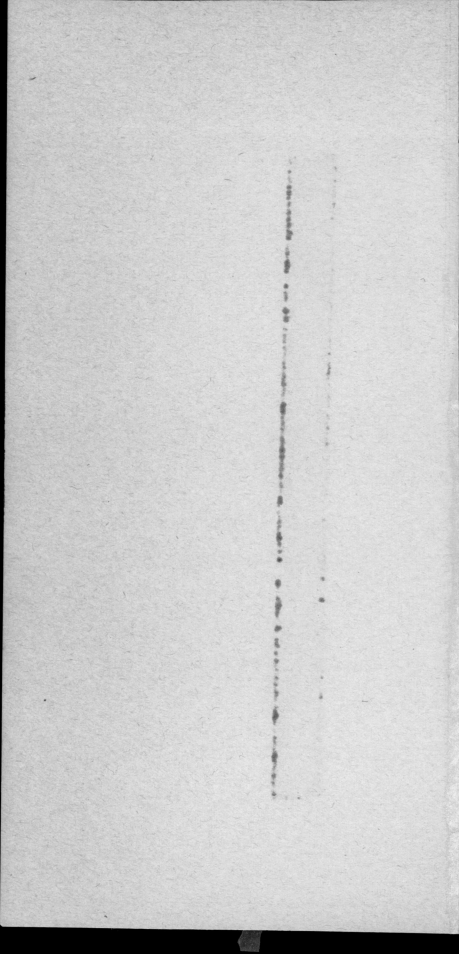

A TREASURY
OF IRISH SAINTS

JOHN IRVINE

A TREASURY OF
IRISH SAINTS

with drawings by
RUTH BRANDT

THE DOLMEN PRESS

Set in Erhardt and Janson types and printed and published by Liam Miller at the Dolmen Press Ltd. 23 Upper Mount Street Dublin 2 in the Republic of Ireland.

First Published: 1964

Distributed outside Ireland by Oxford University Press

NIHIL OBSTAT: Jacobus Hendley, *Cens. Dep.*
IMPRIMATUR: ✠ Daniel, *Epus. Dunen et Connoren.*
Belfast, die 2a Octobris 1958

for

Dorothy Parke

*As a token of a long friendship
and in appreciation of many
lovely musical settings.*

*"There is not enough darkness in all the
world to put out one small candle."*

ACKNOWLEDGMENTS

My thanks are due to the following, for kind permission to reprint poems which first appear-ed in their respective publications:
"The Capuchin Annual" *and* "The Cross".

"A Rathlin Cradle Song", *the musical setting of which is by Dr. Havelock Nelson, is reprint-ed by permission of Messrs Bayley and Ferguson, Ltd., Glasgow.* "The Little Pets of St. Mochua" *also a setting by Dr. Nelson, is now reprinted by permission of Messrs. Augener Ltd., London.*

CONTENTS

SAINT PATRICK

When darkness lay across the land
Saint Patrick lit the Paschal flame
And kindled in the hearts of men
A veneration for the name
Of God, and Jesus Christ His Son,
Who freely gave His life away
And by the shedding of His blood
Redeemed all men at Calvary.

And so they turned from ancient ways,
The pagan gods, the wicked strife,
To hear the creed of gentleness
The promise of eternal life,
And 'ere Saint Patrick's task was done
His converts travelled far and wide
Until the Christian bell was heard
To sound in every countryside

SAINT PATRICK AND
THE SERPENTS

There were serpents once in Ireland
Long centuries ago
In the meadows and the forests
Where men were loth to go.

By Saint Patrick they were banished
Beyond the Irish shore
And one was never seen again
From Slemish to Cahore.

SAINT PATRICK AND
THE SHAMROCK

Saint Patrick held the shamrock
Aloft for all to see
And said "Behold this symbol
Of the Holy Trinity
Of Father, Son, and Holy Ghost,
One, yet one in three."

INVOCATION TO
SAINT BRIDE

Dear Saint Brigid of The Kine
Bless these little fields of mine,
The pastures and the shady trees,
Bless the butter and the cheese,
Bless the cows with coats of silk
And the brimming pails of milk,
Bless the hedgerows, and I pray
Bless the seed beneath the clay,
Bless the hay and bless the grass,
Bless the seasons as they pass,
And heaven's blessings will prevail,
Brigid—Mary of the Gael.

THREE IRISH SAINTS

In Downpatrick on the hill
Saint Patrick, Bride, and Colm-Cille,
Underneath a leafy shade
In one grave at last were laid.

Saint Patrick guard us from all wrong
Let our faith in Christ be strong,
Saint Bride make clean our hearts and
    bless,
And fill them with thy holiness,
Saint Colm, comfort them that stray
And toil in exile far away
From everything that once was dear
In far-off places year by year,
For love of Ireland bless us still,
Saint Patrick, Bride, and Colm-Cille.

SAINT COLM-CILLE AND
THE CAIRN OF FAREWELL

I will not climb these heights again,
For there are thoughts I would not
    wake,
Nor gaze across the sunlit seas
For fear my heart should break.

The oaks are green in Derry now,
The waves break on the Irish shore,
My grief that I must say farewell—
Farewell for evermore . . .

So dear to me the singing birds,
The emerald fields of Innisfail,
What matter where my head shall lie
A blessing on the Gael

The white gulls tumble in the spray
And fill the air with bitter cries,
And wild the tumult of my heart
The longing in my eyes

But row me to Iona's Isle
Though I am weary of the sea,
Beyond the far enpurpled hills
That will not let me be.

*On leaving Ireland, Colm-Cille first
landed upon the little isle of Oronsay, but
on climbing a height, he found that he
could still see his native land. Immediately
he took to his boat and settled at last on
Iona only when he had satisfied himself
that the Green Isle could be seen no more.
A cairn was raised where he first landed
on Oronsay and it is still known as The
Cairn of Farewell.*

[15]

SAINT COLM-CILLE, BROTHER DIARMUID, AND THE CRANE

Three days hence I bid thee wait
Westward of the island, late,
Before the dawn lights up the sky,
For suddenly a crane will fly
Storm-driven from the Irish shore
By Autumnal gales that bore
Her, where the whirling currents meet
To fall exhausted at thy feet.

Pray take her to the sheiling there
And give to her thy loving care,
Until three nights have passed away
And she will no longer stay
With us, her little exile o'er
Then let her fly to that sweet shore
Where thou and I first breathed the air,
So I commend her to thy care.

As he foretold it came to pass,
And three days afterwards at Mass
"God bless thee son" Saint Colm said
"May all thy kindness be repaid."
And Diarmuid answered "Would that
    we
Could follow her across that sea,
Perchance the weary wings that glide
Above the Irish countryside
Shall settle when the sun is low
Among the reeds at Drumahoe."

SAINT COLM-CILLE AND
THE OAK TREES

When Saint Colm-Cille was young
And carefree in his native land,
The blackbird and the thrush would
   come
Betimes and sing upon his hand.

And as he sat beneath the oaks
Before his heart was touched with grief,
He said that God so loved these trees
An angel dwelt in every leaf.

SAINT FIACRE
Patron Saint of Gardeners

Kind Saint! who loved the garden
    flowers,
Be not unmindful of the hours
Spent in unremitting toil
To trim the hedges, break the soil,
And work with clippers, trowels, or
    rakes
Until every muscle aches.

May the slips and bulbs and seeds
Grow more bountiful, rank weeds
Be eaten up when summer brings
Snails, and flies, and creepy things,
And let the borders and the shrubs
Be colourful, and free from grubs.

May the leafy branches spread
A pleasant shelter overhead,
From the sun's persistent rays
In the hot midsummer days,
And when flowers droop and pass,
May colour linger on the grass
When trees do weep their tears of gold,
For Nature's gifts are manifold.

SAINT KEVIN AND
THE ANGEL

An angel to Saint Kevin came
And blessed him by the Holy Name,
Then gazing round him where he stood
At the darkling solitude
To Saint Kevin he did say
"I would sweep these hills away,
Crags and rocks, and wooded dells
Where little grows and no one dwells,
And give you pastures lush and green
For kine to graze, a winding stream,
And gentle fields to grow your grain
In place of this unsought domain."

Saint Kevin slowly shook his head
And kneeling by the lake-side said
"I humbly pray you let them stand,
The rugged hills, the broken land
For I do love like any child

[21]

The hunted creatures of the wild,
And every bird that climbs the sky
Is free to wander just as I
Or dwell in peace beside the lake,
To make them homeless for *my* sake
Would grieve me sorely night and day."
The angel sighed and flew away.

SAINT KEVIN AND
THE WILD BEASTS

Where Kevin was the eagles came
Down from the highest mountains,
   tame,
And sat among the lesser birds
To hear the wisdom of his words,
The speckled trout would swiftly glide
To the reedy water's side,
And there the mountain deer would
   stand
To eat the green moss from his hand,
The snarling wolf and savage boar
Lay down together by his door
And so defied all natural laws
About the cave where Kevin was.

THE LITTLE PETS OF
SAINT MOCHUA

When Saint Mochua knelt to pray
Each morning at the break of day
There always was about the house
A rooster, fly and little mouse,
Three willing slaves to serve him well
And share his solitary cell.
The rooster every morn would crow
And waken him for matins, though
When he slept too sound to hear
The mouse came forth and nipped his
    ear,
And though he never had a clock
The mouse would call him, or the cock,
And if he had to leave a book
From out some dusty hidden nook,
A fly with patience and with grace
Would sit for hours and mark the place.

A RATHLIN CRADLE SONG

The night is on the dark sea wave
And the boats are on the deep,
But here within the quiet room
My treasure lies asleep.
Oh! may Our Lady come and bless
The cradle where you lie,
And wind and wave, and moon and
    stars,
Shall sing you lullaby.

The woodland birds are silent now,
And the empty fields are still.
Night in her sable vestment walks
Across the lonely hill.
Oh! may Our Lady stoop to rock
The cradle where you lie,
And wind and wave, and moon and
    stars,
Shall sing you lullaby.

Husheen! my own, my heart's desire
For the dark earth is at rest,
And there is neither doubt nor sin
In thy untroubled breast.
Oh! may Our Lady's arms enfold
The cradle where you lie,
And wind and wave, and moon and
   stars,
Shall sing you lullaby.

SAINT FINBARR'S HERMITAGE
Gougane Barra

The peace of God enfolds it
And he who tarries there
Shall find a heaven for his eyes,
And in his heart, a prayer.

But he who hurries onwards
May search the world in vain
And never find before he dies,
Such peace on earth again.

EXPLANATORY AND
BIOGRAPHICAL NOTES

St. Patrick Apostle of Ireland

5th century: Feast day March 17th

Lives of the great apostle of Ireland are in
the hands of all, and his writings have again
and again been published and translated.
There is a controversy as to the date and place
of his birth. In his sixteenth year he was carri-
ed into captivity together with other slaves
of his father Calphurnius, and taken to
Ireland. Here "he was admonished in vision
of his future work". Escaping from his cap-
tors, he travelled through Britain, Gaul and
Italy, and in Rome received his mission from
Pope Celestine (A.D. 423-432). Coming to
Ireland, he devoted himself entirely to the
work thus set him. He converted numberless
heathens to Christianity and by establishing
various Bishoprics and holding several Coun-
cils, organized the Church in Ireland. He was
buried at Down in Ulster, but his titular See
he had long before fixed at Armagh. According to seventh century tradition, he died at
Saul on March 17th, 461.

page 10
St. Patrick and the Serpents

*also see note on page 37. St. Finbarr's
Hermitage*

page 11
St. Patrick and the Shamrock

It is interesting to note that early in the
seventeenth century the coinage of King
Charles I depicted St. Patrick with mitre and
crozier, and displaying a trefoil.

St. Bridgid, Bridget, Bride
Mary of the Gael
6th century: Feast day February 1st.

Born of Christian parents in County Louth, which at that time was part of the province of Ulster, about the middle of the fifth century. Her parents are said to have been baptized by St. Patrick himself. She founded the monastery of Kildare, the first religious house of women in Ireland. Wonderful were the miracles she wrought, and equally marvellous her influence for good over the church of her country. Her remains were enshrined with those of St. Patrick, as being the relics of the Second Patron Saint of Ireland. In art, St. Bride is represented holding a cross—with a flame over her head—sometimes with a cow near her, she being reputed the Protectoress of those engaged in dairy work.

'Brigid our torch our sun,
The pure virgin whom we love
Worthy of honour without end.'

Kildare (Kill Dara) means the cell of the oak, and it was there that St. Brigid had her first cell built under a great oak tree.

January 31st., the eve of St. Brigid, was once known in rural Ireland as Oidhe na Cruha, the night of the crosses. Within living memory the following beautiful custom was observed by the peasantry.

Oaten cakes were baked and dried before the open hearth fire while the potatoes were being boiled for the supper. Out of doors a large sheaf of green rushes rested against the wall. When the daily tasks had been finished, all knelt for the family Rosary in honour of the Saint, then, the eldest member would go out to carry in the rushes, first knocking on the door and saying three times, "Open your eyes and hearts, and allow St. Brigid to enter".

Those inside, on bended knees, would then reverently reply three times, "Welcome, O Welcome, good St. Brigid", this was all spoken in the native tongue. Next, the supper was served of "poundies" (mashed potatoes), and the oaten cakes. After the meal everyone would sit round the fire making St. Brigid crosses. Some of them to be kept in the home, others for the barns, byres, and stables. A few single rushes would be knotted together, to be kept in case of headaches, toothaches, or other illness of any member of the family during the year.

When eventually bedtime came, the last to retire would gather up what remained of the scattered rushes, and lay them in front of the still warm hearthstone. These were to be a bed for the Saint to rest in if she chanced to enter during the hours of darkness when all were asleep.

page 13
Three Irish Saints

An old story tells how St. Colm-Cille was first buried on Iona but his grave on the island was violated by Viking raiders. They even plundered the graves in the cemetery searching for treasure that might have been left with the dead, and the coffin of Colm-Cille was taken out of its tomb and put on the ship of a raider whose name was Mandan. The raiders hoped to find within the oak coffin another one of silver. On opening it, there being no silver, only a body wondrously preserved, they closed the coffin and consigned it to the waves. Though Mandan's ship was far from Ireland when this was done, the coffin floated across the sea and through many channels until it landed on the Irish shore. There it was found by peasants who brought it to the

Abbot of Down. He ordered the coffin to be opened and great was his astonishment, and thankfulness to find certain writings by which it was established that the body was that of St. Colm-Cille. On the orders of the Abbot, the Saint was buried in the tomb that was St. Patrick's and St. Brigid's.

page 14
St. Colm-Cille and the Cairn of Farewell
6th century: Feast day June 9th

Colm-Cille, called Columba, the latinized version of his name by the Scots. Originally baptized by the name of Colm (The Dove) and later to distinguish him from other Saints of that name Colm-Cille from the great number of monastic cells (called by the Irish "Killes") of which he was the founder. He was born in County Donegal and had a most passionate love for his own country. After a dispute, he left Ireland as a self-inflicted penance and founded the great monastery at Iona where he died. St. Adamhnán, who wrote his biography, tells us that Colm-Cille could think of no penance more severe than the one that had been inflicted on himself, and for long after the event, he could not bring himself to pronounce the name of Ireland.

page 16
St. Colm-Cille, Brother Diarmuid and the Crane

An instance which shows the great compassion of the Saint, and his undying love for Ireland.

page 18
St. Colm-Cille and the Oak Trees

It is clear from the writing of St. Colm-Cille

[34]

that above all earthly things he loved Derry
(Doire: The oak grove), and the trees from
which it took its name.

"For heaven's angels come and go
Under every leaf of the oaks,
I love my beautiful Derry"

page 19
St. Fiacre: Patron Saint of Gardeners

St. Fiacre is claimed both by the Scots and
the Irish as their countryman. He crossed to
Gaul early in the sixth century and being
kindly received by St. Faro, Bishop of Meaux,
he thenceforth lived the life of an anchorite
in a neighbouring forest.

As Patron of gardeners, he is often represented as carrying a spade. The Paris cabs took
the name of 'fiacres' from having started
from a house with a statue of this Saint over
the doorway.

page 21
St. Kevin and the Angel
7th century: Feast day June 3rd

When an angel came to Kevin at Glendaloch
and offered to level the high mountains around
his retreat, the Saint was shocked at the sugges-
tion and said, "I have no desire that any
creature of God should be moved or disturbed
because of me."

page 23
St. Kevin and the Wild Beasts

When St. Kevin was at Glendaloch not even
the fiercest of the wild beasts ever disputed
his right to be there nor by any harsh or
impatient deed did he ever dispute theirs.

[35]

The Little Pets of St. Mochua
6th century

". . . When Mochua who was likewise known by the name of Mac Duath, retired into the wilderness for the benefit of his devotion, he had no living creatures about him except a cock, a mouse, and a fly . . ." This Irish Saint was closely associated with St. Colm-Cille and is reputed to have visited him at the great monastery of Iona.

When his three treasures died it is said that he wrote to St. Colm-Cille bemoaning the loss of his little flock.

Colm-Cille in his reply said, "Brother you need scarcely be surprised at the death of the flock that you have lost, for there is no misfortune except where wealth is."

By this joking of real Saints it is clear that they were not much interested in worldly goods, unlike most people of our time.

A Rathlin Cradle Song

Rathlin island lies off the North East corner of County Antrim, and the first Christian church there was founded by St. Comgall of Bangor.

According to tradition it was here that Robert Bruce, the hero of Bannockburn, observed the spider and took courage from its patience and persistence.

To this day a crumbling ruin there is known as Bruce's castle.

St. Finbarr's Hermitage

St. Finbarr 6th century :
Feast day September 25th

The following interesting note appears in
"Murray's Handbook of Ireland" 1878
"St. Patrick after banishing the reptiles out
of the country overlooked one hideous
monster, a winged dragon, which desolated
the adjacent country, and power was conferr-
ed on a holy man, Fineen Bar, to drown the
monster in Gougane lake, on condition of
his erecting a church where its waters met
the tide, and the Saint, having exterminated
the monster, fulfilled the agreement by found-
ing the present Cathedral of Cork."

A DOLMEN PRESS BOOK

Printed in the Republic of Ireland